S0-CWS-971

beginnings

the spiritual life

Small-Group Leader's Guide

Andy Langford, Mark Ralls,
and Rob Weber

Abingdon Press / Nashville

Beginnings: The Spiritual Life
Small-Group Leader's Guide

Copyright © 2006 by Abingdon Press.

This book is printed on acid-free, elemental chlorine-free paper.

ISBN 0-687-33054-8

06 07 08 09 10 11 12 13 14 15 — 10 9 8 7 6 5 4 3 2 1

MANUFACTURED IN THE UNITED STATES OF AMERICA

Contents

Introduction   5

Part One: Preparing for *The Spiritual Life*   7

1. Welcome to *The Spiritual Life*   9
2. Small-Group Leaders   10
    Why Were You Chosen as a Small-Group Leader?
    Preliminary Details
    Leading Your Small Group:
       Be Open to the Leading of the Holy Spirit
    Your Gifts as a Small-Group Leader
    Leadership Skills
    Small-Group Helpers
    Summary
3. The Program   19
    Training Session
    The Program: Spiritual Habits
    The Audience: People Who Are Spiritually Hungry
    The Goal: Renewing the Heart
    Basic Resources
    Program Characteristics
    Housekeeping Details
    Your Team
    The Weekly Sessions
    Helping Inquirers Follow Jesus Christ
    How Can I Begin an Intentional Journey With Jesus Christ?

Part Two: Leading *The Spiritual Life*
Session Outlines for Small-Group Leaders 31

Session 1: Where Is the Spirit in Spirituality? 33
Introduction to the Spiritual Life

Session 2: How Much Am I Willing to Risk? 37
The Spiritual Habit of Courage

Session 3: What Is Most Important to Me? 41
The Spiritual Habit of Loving

Session 4: Can I Find Balance in a Whirlwind World? 45
The Spiritual Habit of Centering

Session 5: What Do I Want to Be When I Grow Up? 49
The Spiritual Habit of Simplicity

Session 6: How Do I Keep My Possessions From Possessing Me? 53
The Spiritual Habit of Giving

Session 7: How Do I Get Ahead? 57
The Spiritual Habit of Serving

Session 8: Can I Go Deeper Without Going Under? 61
The Spiritual Habit of Trusting

Session 9: What Do I Do With My Doubts? 65
The Spiritual Habit of Questioning

Session 10: Can a Change in Me Change the World? 69
The Spiritual Habit of Engaging

Introduction

The Spiritual Life: Small-Group Leader's Guide is the resource for small-group discussion leaders in congregations that are offering *The Spiritual Life.* This resource is used in conjunction with

- *The Spiritual Life: Director's Manual,* the key organizational resource;
- *The Spiritual Life: Video Resources,* a set of presentations by Rob Weber that introduce a Christian perspective on developing some basic spiritual habits;
- *The Spiritual Life: Participant's Guide,* a workbook for program participants;
- *The Spiritual Life: Habits of the Heart,* a book that is the foundation of and expands upon the video presentations.

Part One:

Preparing for
The Spiritual Life

1.

Welcome to
The Spiritual Life

Welcome to the ten sessions of *The Spiritual Life*. We believe these next few weeks could be very important for you and for the people you will lead. Each week you will guide a group of inquirers who are asking fundamental questions about the spiritual life. With your guidance, they will explore who they are, who God is, and how our lives intersect with God.

In each session all participants will see and hear Rob Weber talking about a biblical story that helps us understand a spiritual habit of the Christian life. Small groups will then gather for discussion led by you and, if your group is larger than ten persons, by other members of your leadership team.

Each of us is a work in progress, and in these times together you may discover some serious work going on. These few weeks may change the lives of some people, including possibly your own. Together women and men will discover who Christians believe the Holy Spirit is; how God's Spirit touches our lives; and how our relationship with God may be strengthened through specific Christian spiritual habits such as loving, giving, questioning, and serving.

As you share with your group members some of the basic beliefs and spiritual practices of the Christian faith, you will be inviting fellow spiritual beggars on a journey of discovery. We call this journey a spiritual quest. Like the sower in Jesus' parable, you will scatter the seeds of the good news of Jesus Christ upon all sorts of ground—some rocky, some thin, some covered with weeds, and some that is fertile. We then leave it to the work of the Holy Spirit to determine what will take root and grow (Luke 8:4-8).

Welcome, sower, to the journey!

2.

Small-Group Leaders

The small-group community you lead in *The Spiritual Life* is the most important component of this entire program. Your discussion, which follows Rob Weber's video/DVD presentation each week, invites all the participants into a deeper relationship with one another; with your congregation; and, most importantly, with the Holy Spirit. Just as Jesus chose twelve ordinary people to be his first followers, so Jesus promised that he is present whenever two or three persons are gathered together in his name (Matthew 18:20). You are the host of this Christ-centered gathering.

WHY WERE YOU CHOSEN AS A SMALL-GROUP LEADER?

As a discussion leader, you guide all the participants toward Jesus Christ.
In this task you are acting like Jesus' first disciple, Simon Peter. In the Gospel of Mark, the first words of Jesus to Simon the fisherman were, "Follow me . . . and I will send you out to fish for people" (Mark 1:17). Then, in John's Gospel, Jesus' last words to Simon, now called Peter the Rock, were to "feed" and "take care of" the people of God (John 21:15-19). We believe that you, like Simon Peter, have a personal relationship with Jesus Christ and a desire to share your spiritual quest with other people. You truly are the Peter-like companion on the journey for every participant in your small group. We believe that you have the God-given gifts and talents to serve in this role.

PRELIMINARY DETAILS

Your weekly task begins at the start of each session. You are the hospitable host who welcomes each participant, and especially the persons who are in your small group. Over a meal or refreshments, your job is to help people feel welcome by learning their names and listening to their stories. Essentially, you are meeting some new people who may well become your companions in our Christian faith.

After the meal/refreshments and gathering time, everyone watches a video/DVD presentation about a basic spiritual habit. In each session all participants will see and hear Rob Weber talking about a biblical story that helps us understand a spiritual habit of the Christian life. At the end of the presentation, you will guide the members of your small group in a discussion of the presentation and the questions they have.

Your small group should include between six and twelve people (including you and any helpers you have). Up to one-third of your small group, including you, may be hosts helping with the program.

If there is more than one small group in the program, your director will assign you to a space that your group will occupy each week. At the first few meetings, there will be a sign with your name or group number that identifies your group's space. Your group should sit in a circle or around a table. Everyone should be able to see the face of everyone else clearly and to hear plainly. Encourage people to rotate where they sit so that they will sit next to and meet someone new at each session. At the end of the session, if requested, straighten up the room and put away the chairs and other materials.

You have been designated as the small-group leader. Another person may have been designated as your primary assistant, and possibly one or two other persons in your group have been designated as helpers. You and your primary assistant should definitely come to the opening organizational meeting that takes place a few minutes before the sessions begin every week.

If there is more than one small group in the program, your director will assign participants to your small group. We hope that all participants will find other people in your group who are similar to them. No one wants to be the odd person out. Recognize that there is high stress in joining a new group in which most people are strangers. If a person is uncomfortable in your group, he or she probably will not come back. If you discover that someone wishes to move to a different group, talk with your director and make a change by the next meeting without creating a major fuss.

LEADING YOUR SMALL GROUP:
Be Open to the Leading of the Holy Spirit

How do you accompany the participants in your group on this journey? Your goal as a discussion leader is to enable spiritual growth along God's way by each group member. Your task is to encourage each person to understand and to be open to the grace of God in her or his own life. Even though the group members have heard the same content through the presentation, the basis for your group discussion is not "What did Rob Weber intend to say?" but "What did you hear in this biblical story and presentation that connects to your life or illuminates your experiences?" The questions we provide for each session will assist you with this work, but our experience is that people are eager to talk as soon as the presentation is over. The members of your small group simply need a wise guide to shape their conversation.

In light of this approach, you do not need to provide "correct" answers to questions. Instead, you are to create an environment where possible answers are explored and additional questions may be asked. In response to these presentations, a good discussion is not a debate about any particular person's ideas but a mutual sharing of experiences and opinions. Even though your group members will have heard the same presentation, your group discussions may move in unexpectedly different directions. Do your best to be open to the movement of the Holy Spirit and to be vigilant in discerning the difference between following the Spirit's lead and going off on a side road. Working in partnership with the Holy Spirit (called the "Guide" in this resource), who alone can bring about spiritual transformation, you may achieve marvelous things. Your success as a small-group leader will not be judged by what your group members "know" by the end of this program but by the way their lives are changed in the months and years to come.

In summary, you will read and study each week the material in this SMALL-GROUP LEADER'S GUIDE and the accompanying book, *Habits of the Heart: A Participant's Companion;* watch and listen to the video/DVD presentations along with the participants in your small group; and facilitate your participants in sharing with the group. You may lead by offering your own honest reflections, but you will be even more successful if you enable your group members to listen carefully to one another and to the Holy Spirit. You are the one who leads your participants in a movement from the head to the heart to the hands and feet.

YOUR GIFTS AS A SMALL-GROUP LEADER

Leading small groups requires particular gifts and skills. As you guide the small-group members toward Jesus Christ, you need a variety of God-given gifts, including patience, care, support, encouragement, openness, silence, peace, and prayer. In addition, you should be fully prepared for each session, gently guide the conversation, avoid fixing problems, and watch the clock. When you exhibit these gifts and skills, all the participants can have confidence in their guide and companion in the way toward Jesus Christ.

1. Patience is among the qualities that you need most as a discussion leader. Be patient, and let the Holy Spirit guide the process. While you may wish for rapid success, remember that the development of a relationship with Jesus Christ is a lifelong process. It may be difficult to identify any great leap on any particular day, but over time God is at work in the life of every person. Trust the work of the Holy Spirit as you meet with your small group.

2. Care for each person in your small group. Good shepherds watch carefully over each of their sheep. The aim of *The Spiritual Life* is that every single woman and man should be nurtured, which is why you have multiple congregational hosts in your small group. After the first session, assign one of your small-group hosts to take responsibility for two or three of the participants in your small group. Care can be shown in a number of ways. For example, if one of your participants misses a meeting, it is your responsibility to check and be sure nothing is wrong. Be careful, however, not to be too aggressive in this shepherding. It is appropriate to call participants on the phone or send an e-mail if they miss a session and to express concern and offer appropriate support. If someone was sick, send a get-well card and provide a summary of what happened in the session. If someone did not have transportation, offer to arrange a ride. It is, however, inappropriate to call a participant and berate her or him for missing a session. If someone wants to end the relationship or stop attending the sessions, let him or her go with a prayer. This system of one-on-one care is one of the most crucial aspects of *The Spiritual Life.*

3. Support spiritual growth. While spiritual maturity cannot develop overnight, you can assist your participants through the early stages of their walk and later help integrate them into a congregational group once they have completed *The Spiritual Life.* In general, you should tend to be more active earlier in the program, when people do not know one another well, and then back away as your group matures. Be attuned to the interests of your group members so that once they have completed *The Spiritual Life,* you are prepared to guide them to other experiences within your congregation. If participants within your group who are not members of your congregation start attending worship services in your church, arrange to meet and sit with them. Also encourage them to become involved in various congregational activities.

Part of encouraging spiritual maturity is to help participants avoid attaching themselves to any leader other than Jesus Christ. For example, good parents begin by feeding their children; but as the children grow, mature parents teach their children to feed themselves. Beware of any unhealthy dependence by any of your participants upon any leader. Instead, encourage your group members to grow in their relationships with a variety of people within the weekly gatherings and maybe within your congregation. Your small group is the ideal place to start developing such friendships.

4. Encourage. In the early church, Barnabas and the apostles encouraged Paul. In response, Paul urged new Christians to "encourage one another and build each other up" (1 Thessalonians 5:11). In our modern society, negative criticism dominates our political and cultural environment, which often leads to fear, insecurity, trepidation, and timidity. People may shrivel up or close down in a too critical atmosphere, yet everyone can flourish in an atmosphere of encouragement. For example, you and your helpers should strive to find ways to affirm each participant each week.

There are many ways to encourage participants, especially those who are unrelated to your congregation. A key way of encouragement is for you to begin to know each person well. Start by learning all the participants' names. Write down everyone's name at the first session, pray for the people by name each day during the week, and call each person by name during the second session. Throughout the program, smile at people and express warmth and responsiveness to every participant, especially to those who are not members of your congregation.

Encouragement also involves the gift of engaging others in conversation. Especially try to foster contributions from the quieter members of your group. If one person has done a lot of talking, ask, "What do the rest of you think?" In addition, ask simple, open-ended questions, such as, "What do you think?" and "How do you feel?" and "What has been your experience?" Instead of asking questions that can be answered with either a "Yes" or "No," ask questions that provoke discussion, such as, "How does this story match your experiences?" As a small-group leader you typically should not answer your own questions; if people seem reluctant to answer, try rephrasing. If someone asks you a question that you cannot answer, be honest and say, "I don't know, but I will try to find out by next week."

Remember that all contributions by each member in your small group have value. Even when a group member says something that may appear wrong or silly, positive ways of responding might include, "How interesting!" or "That's a new idea I've never considered!" Create an environment in which your group members can say what they think without fear of embarrassment or ridicule. Involving everyone means taking seriously the ideas, opinions, and insights of each person.

Involvement, however, does not always require speaking. Some people actively participate simply by listening. Grant every person in your group the right to be silent or to say, "Pass" when a question is asked. Silence can be golden. Do not insist that introverts become extroverts. All of these techniques will result in a group whose members understand you as an encourager.

5. Listen. The Letter of James states, "Be quick to listen, slow to speak" (James 1:19). In your small group, speak softly and listen intently. If participants have ideas that are odd or strange, do not respond too quickly (as if their ideas are not even worth considering) or correct them. First, listen. Then try to understand these persons' perspectives or feelings. Finally, show respect. Because listening is more important than speaking, you should not force your own ideas on the group. If someone directly asks you for your own view, answer briefly and then redirect the question to other participants.

6. Keep confidentiality. Assure the members of your small group that their personal stories or issues stay within the group. While your small group may not be bound by rules regarding pastoral confidentiality, gossip and inappropriate conversation outside the group will destroy relationships that are forming. At your first session, insist that people listen carefully to one another and then keep in confidence what is shared in the group. If you perceive that a participant has a particular need or is involved in a crisis, you may wish to share this concern in general with your pastor in a way that does not break confidence.

7. Be a peacemaker. Be gracious, and avoid getting into arguments. Encourage everyone to follow the old Southern saying, "You do not have to like anyone, but you must be courteous to everyone." People rarely change their mind after they get involved in an argument, especially if the disagreement is about religion. It is easy to win an argument and lose a person. If an argument begins, quickly reconcile differences or acknowledge that there are different legitimate opinions. Tears, fears, and anger may all be part of this process; but neither you nor anyone else should dictate how other people respond. Truth is important, but speak the truth in love.

These seven positive qualities—patience, caring, building, encouraging, listening, keeping confidences, and peacemaking—will ensure your success as a small-group leader. When you exhibit these qualities, the way will be smooth.

LEADERSHIP SKILLS

There are a number of leadership skills that you will also use:

1. Be prepared. If you are not properly prepared, your discussion will flounder. Each week, review the material to be presented; read the appropriate chapter in *Habits of the Heart: A Participant's Companion;* answer the questions for yourself; evaluate your own leadership the previous week; consider each participant and his or her own needs and expectations; and then be ready to lead.

2. Guide the conversation gently. For example, if a participant becomes too dominant, be willing, for the sake of the whole group, to intervene gently by saying, "What do others of you think?" or speak with the person after adjournment. Permitting one participant to dominate, for the sake of avoiding conflict, can have a harmful effect on your discussion. On the opposite side, if you are an excessively dominant leader, you may kill dialogue by doing all the talking instead of giving the participants the freedom to speak and to say what is on their mind. Do not see yourself as an expert with an appropriate response to whatever anyone says; that is, do not dominate the conversation. Silence is okay. In general, if you speak for more than five minutes of the discussion, you have spoken too much. Patience and listening are the needed skills.

3. Avoid fixing individual problems. When someone presents a specific problem to your group, it is tempting for you and others in the group to want to find a solution and fix the problem. Problem solving can make you and other people feel better, wiser, and more powerful; but fixing is not helping. Instead, share your own experiences and let the participants find their own solutions. Also, avoid attempting to convince everyone to follow someone else's personal path. It is far more useful to be able to clarify and celebrate someone else's experience than to urge another person to try to duplicate another's unique experience.

4. Keep a sense of time. Watch the clock, and keep to the schedule. Keep your discussion to the set time. Also, make sure that your group does not spend too much time on a minor question and, as a result, have less time to spend on deeper questions that you know will arise later in the session. Finally, the session should not extend beyond the adjournment time, even if the group members are involved in a lively discussion. It is better to say, "Let's continue this next week," which encourages people to return to continue the dialogue. The danger in going beyond the adjournment time is that some people may hesitate to come back, fearing another late adjournment. If persons wish to stay and continue the conversation, however, you and your helpers should make yourselves available until each participant is ready to leave.

5. Pray. The greatest gift you must have is the gift of prayer. Pray for your small group and for each participant every day. Begin this pattern at the end of your first discussion in the first week by closing the session with prayer. As the small-group leader, take the lead in this prayer, especially in the first few weeks. Your prayers should be brief. If you offer long, poetic prayers, this may hinder other people in the group from offering their own tentative prayers.

As the weeks pass, you may want to invite other members of your group to pray; but be careful not to put anyone on the spot. If you ask participants to pray, instead of asking them spontaneously in front of everyone else, ask them prior to the session so they will have a chance to prepare. If persons are not experienced in praying in public, you may suggest a simple prayer, such as, "Will you ask God to watch over us this next week?" Because many people find praying out loud very difficult, you may wish to introduce a simple prayer model, such as, "Almighty God, (a short petition for each person in your group). We pray in Jesus' name. Amen." Be sensitive to people's feelings, and do not pressure anyone to pray aloud who does not want to do so.

In conclusion, as a small-group leader you need, and God will provide for you, a host of spiritual gifts and leadership skills. When you truly care for the participants and welcome all of them into your community through all your words and actions, God will change lives. Even more so, you who have befriended these persons will also be blessed by God.

SMALL-GROUP HELPERS

In your small discussion group, you may also have one-to-three helpers, preferably a mix of women and men. Your helpers need to have the same spiritual qualities and gifts as you. They also may be former participants who just finished a previous program of the *Beginnings* series.

One of your helpers may be a small-group leader in training or an assistant discussion leader. Serving as a helper is the best way for a person to receive training to be a small-group leader or to serve in some other position the next time the program is offered. There may be occasions when you must miss a session or need special help to bring a discussion back to focus. There may also be times when a group member needs some extra help. This job may be a task you assign to your primary assistant.

If you must miss a session, ask one of your helpers, a person whom the other members know and trust, to lead that session. Ideally, meet with your helper and supply a copy of all the appropriate material. Go over the general outline of the presentation and the discussion questions. Draw on any particular knowledge you have about any of the participants that may be helpful but does not violate confidentiality. Give special attention to preparation details, such as set-up and the closing prayer.

Helpers must understand, however, that their role is to help, not to lead or to dominate. Helpers, sometimes because of their own experiences, may wish to use your small group as a sounding board. Most of the conversation, however, must come from the guest participants, not from the small-group leaders and helpers. Assist your helpers in resisting the temptation to speak first or to speak often. Certainly encourage them not to talk for more than about five minutes of the total discussion time.

SUMMARY

Your small group, the heart of *The Spiritual Life,* brings inquirers into relationship with one another; with your congregation as a whole; and, most importantly, with Jesus Christ. Your leadership of your small group may well serve as the catalyst to fundamental Christian formation for these persons. May God bless your work.

3.

The Program

In the *Beginnings* program, we seek to fulfill the church's ancient task of sharing the gospel feast. *Beginnings: An Introduction to Christian Faith* provides the "first course" of this feast, introducing twelve core beliefs and practices related to Jesus Christ. Throughout that first course, we invite inquirers to begin an intentional journey with Jesus Christ. At the end of the first course, we hope that participants will make a decision to explore the Christian life more deeply. Then, what comes next? We believe that participants, having been introduced to Jesus Christ, will ask, "What are the spiritual characteristics of someone who follows Jesus Christ?"

TRAINING SESSION

Your director will conduct the training session for *The Spiritual Life*. It is vital for you to participate in this session. This training session is usually held the week prior to the start of the program on the same day and hours that the program will be conducted.

The following topics are discussed in the training session: the nature of this program, the people we are trying to reach, and our motivation in sharing this ministry. The training session also focuses on the practical details that will enable this program to succeed: the various resources available, key elements of the program, basic housekeeping details that involve your participation, the tasks of various team members, and an outline of a typical session.

THE PROGRAM:
SPIRITUAL HABITS

Beginnings: The Spiritual Life assists persons both inside and outside the church in answering the question, "What are the spiritual characteristics of someone who follows Jesus Christ?" It offers a "second course" in the gospel feast. *The Spiritual Life* explores ten habits of Christian spirituality, such as love, faith, simplicity, stewardship, and even doubt. In this course, we tie each of these habits to the power of the Holy Spirit or Guide working within us and invite participants to continue their own spiritual journey or quest.

The Spiritual Life, like all *Beginnings* programs, has a number of distinctive characteristics:

1. Everyone is welcome.
2. Our program is direct and clear.
3. The Bible is our core resource.
4. Our theology is consistent with mainline, Protestant Christianity.
5. Our style is one of gracious invitation.
6. Our illustrations are diverse, and our language is inclusive.
7. Our program is simple.
8. We emphasize your congregational setting.
9. We appeal to person's hearts and heads.
10. Our program fits the lifestyles of newcomers and new generations.

THE AUDIENCE:
PEOPLE WHO ARE SPIRITUALLY HUNGRY

Our primary mission in *The Spiritual Life* is to assist you in inviting inquirers, as well as long-standing members of your church, into a deeper relationship with Jesus Christ by sharing the spiritual habits of the Christian life. Who are these persons? They are the women and men who live in your neighborhood, work in your office, belong to your health club, attend your P.T.A. meetings, worship at your church, and are part of your extended family. They are people who are beginning to develop the spiritual practices that comprise the Christian life, and the people whom God is inviting into a deeper relationship. In the broadest sense, every one of us is spiritually hungry.

Among the "inquirers" we intend to reach through this program are seekers, cultural Christians, new believers, and new members of your congregation. Seekers and cultural Christians are those women and men who are not a part of an established Christian or other faith community and yet are on a profound spiritual journey. Seekers know very little about Jesus Christ and have never participated in a Christian community. Cultural Christians are people who know a little about Jesus but have a marginal relationship with your congregation. New Christian believers and new members are beginning their Christian journey and need additional information and encouragement for their walk.

The program is also intended to help you reach out to established church members. We never stop seeking a deeper relationship with God through Jesus Christ. Longtime believers and members of your congregation often ask spiritual questions that are similar to those of persons who are new to the faith, and too often these basic questions go unaddressed. For this reason, *The Spiritual Life* is for all inquirers and is equally suited for those "saints" of your community who are well along their journey to Christian maturity.

THE GOAL:
RENEWING THE HEART

Our goal in *The Spiritual Life* is to redirect women and men toward the way of Jesus Christ. *Redirection* is our word for the first steps in conversion. Because we believe that conversion is a journey that encompasses the whole of a person's life, we do not believe that anyone will experience complete conversion through any one course. We do believe, however, that this program offers the opportunity to choose intentionally a new direction to travel that ultimately leads to the abundant life shared with the Spirit of God.

The Spiritual Life is particularly concerned with redirecting the inner lives of participants toward a deeper relationship with the Holy Spirit. We believe that such redirection can truly be transformative and that it can occur at the deepest part of the self. Traditionally, this core part of the self is described using the metaphor of the heart. The heart is the central and intimate core of our being, the place where we are most truly ourselves. We believe that we need to develop new spiritual habits in order to engage this deepest part of ourselves and then redirect it toward Christ through the power of the Holy Spirit. We believe that this process will be experienced as a renewal of the heart, leaving behind old habits that direct us toward the superficial parts of our lives and initiating new habits that take us both deeper into ourselves and deeper into the heart of God.

This "renewing of the heart" is possible for all Christians, whatever their level of experience. For both new and experienced Christians, God continues to open up unimagined possibilities for growth in grace and ever-new beginnings along the way of Jesus Christ. Thus, one goal of *The Spiritual Life* is to engage new inquirers and experienced Christian inquirers in a shared conversation about the renewal of the heart. We believe that through such holy conversation, participants will be invited to share more deeply in the life of the Spirit.

BASIC RESOURCES

The program consists of five basic resources:

Director's Manual provides the theological background to the program and basic information needed to use *The Spiritual Life* in your congregation. Your director will use this resource.

Video Resources is a series of ten presentations by Rob Weber, each approximately twenty minutes long. These presentations introduce session topics and the corresponding spiritual habits through stories and Scripture.

Small-Group Leader's Guide describes the leader's roles and responsibilities, provides help in organizing and facilitating the small-group sessions, and gives ideas for discussion following the video presentations.

Participant's Guide is the participants' workbook, including reflection questions, activities, and guided journaling. Each participant should have one of these books.

Habits of the Heart: A Participant's Companion is an engaging book that parallels and complements the video resource. This book provides the core biblical story, additional scriptural references, and supplemental illustrations that expand upon the video presentations. We strongly suggest that each participant have a copy of *Habits of the Heart* to use alongside the *Participant's Guide.*

PROGRAM CHARACTERISTICS

The Spiritual Life has a number of key characteristics that are part of each session. Each of the following foundational elements is essential to everyone's positive experience of the program:

1. Inviting
2. Eating
3. Laughing
4. Singing and worshiping
5. Learning
6. Asking
7. Sharing

HOUSEKEEPING DETAILS

At your first group session, your director will provide you with a blank "Contact Sheet" on which to write the following information: name of participant, telephone number, and e-mail address. Understand, however, that this contact information is being collected only for special needs, such as the necessity to inform participants that a session has been canceled or to alert persons about a problem. Turn in your "Contact Sheet" to your director at the end of the first session; your director will make a copy and return the original to you as soon as possible. Do not give each member of your small group or anyone else a copy of the "Contact Sheet." If participants want to exchange addresses and telephone numbers, they may do this individually. If anyone asks you for this information, do not share it under any circumstances. Respect and honor the participants' privacy.

Later in the program, your director will give each participant a "Participant Questionnaire." The information participants provide will help your team evaluate the program and leaders and assist you in planning the next program.

Your director will also give you your own "Small-Group Leader Questionnaire" about your experience with the program. In addition, he or she will give you a copy of the form "Small-Group Leader Evaluation of Participants," which asks you which group members completed the program and if a person did not complete it, as well as why (if you know). This form also asks you to describe briefly how your group members are going to continue their spiritual journey and which participants might serve as helpers during a future program.

Please take these forms seriously and prepare them promptly.

YOUR TEAM

The leadership team for *The Spiritual Life* consists of the servant guides who will be the enablers of the program in your congregation. That is, you and the other members of your team are the companions for inquirers on the way; you are the midwives who make new birth in Jesus Christ possible in the birthing room of your congregation. Your team members are the hands, feet, ears, and mouths of the body of Christ, who make visible to all the participants Jesus Christ himself.

The following persons will manage the various tasks necessary for the program: pastor, director, music/worship leader, meal coordinator, treasurer, you and the other small-group discussion leaders, and small-group helpers.

In programs with a small number of participants, not every task or assignment needs a different person; as few as two people can lead a program for eight other people. The goal is to have the right number of team members so that everyone has a significant role to play but no team member is overwhelmed by her or his responsibilities.

We recommend that, if possible, at least one-third of the participants in the program be from your congregation. This many congregational participants are needed in order to have at least three members from your congregation in each small group. All of your leadership team members need to have an active faith in Jesus Christ. They must be gracious to guests, familiar with Scripture, comfortable with small groups, and attentive to the movement of the Spirit in a group.

Throughout *The Spiritual Life,* you and all the team members will work hard and must have a high level of commitment. Participants will only reach the level of commitment exhibited by everyone on your team. If every member of your leadership team does not attend each session, the participants will be unlikely to do so. Make the serious effort to do the necessary preparation, to attend all the sessions, to talk with participants instead of friends in the congregation, and to concentrate on the task. Occasions will arise when you are unable to attend a session, but this program must be a high priority in your life.

Your pastor, the shepherd of the people of God, is the key to the success of *The Spiritual Life* in your church. As the spiritual guide of a congregation, she or he needs to demonstrate strong, visible, and vocal support of the program, possibly even serving as your director. Please listen to and follow the leadership of your pastor.

Your director must have the gifts of organization and leadership, as well as the ability to speak well in front of a group of participants. He or she has a number of specific responsibilities and may well ask you to assist in a number of ways. Please help in every way requested.

Your music/worship leader uses his or her gift of music to touch people's emotions, proclaim the faith, and point women and men toward God. This ministry may be rather important in your group, or it may be omitted. If there is singing, however, please be an enthusiastic singer. All of the participants will take their cue from you and others on your team.

Your meal coordinator is responsible for the food and all the related activities. Some of your small-group helpers may be recruited to assist in the preparation and serving of the meal. Even if you do not like the food served, thank the meal coordinator after each meal.

Your treasurer keeps all the financial accounts, makes necessary purchases, and assists other team members in purchasing the supplies they need. We suggest that it is best not to charge participants who are not members of your congregation for the program as a whole or for the various parts of the program, such as the weekly meal and materials. You, however, as a congregational host, may be asked to contribute to the meal each week.

Besides being committed to the program itself, you and your team will be involved in follow-up after the program to welcome and possibly incorporate participants into your congregation. Also essential for team members is a commitment to the program in prayer. Pray regularly for every aspect of *The Spiritual Life:* your team as a whole, the meal, the video/DVD presentations, and the individual members of your team. Also commit yourself to pray for every participant in your small group.

Remember, the success of *The Spiritual Life* depends on your team members, who guide each program. When they reach out to their friends, neighbors, family members, coworkers, church members, and inquirers, God will give them the skills they need to share the Lord's banquet with everyone.

Finally, be assured that your program will be successful, not because of the skills of your team members, but because of God's grace. God alone inspires your leaders, the Holy Spirit empowers your team, and the destination is clearly God's kingdom.

THE WEEKLY SESSIONS

The Spiritual Life may be held in the morning, at midday, or in the evening. Your director will share the schedule with you, both for each week and for the whole program. Each program, however, has the following pattern of activities:

At the beginning, before any participants arrive, all your team members gather for a few minutes for organization and prayer. During this time your director guides a brief discussion about the theme of the session and any necessary housekeeping details. You can assist by mentioning other details necessary for the session to go well. This preparation time ends with prayer led by your director. This orientation meeting concludes before the participants begin to arrive so that your team members may go out and welcome the gathering participants. Your task is to go to your table and greet participants when they come to eat with you.

There is a meal. Eating together, especially as a small group, is an essential part of the program. Typically, your small discussion group sits together; and you and your helpers act as hosts and facilitate the conversations. During the meal, there should be no agenda other than encouraging people to visit with one another in a relaxed way. The goal of the meal is for participants to become friends with one another.

Your director now welcomes everyone briefly and describes the focus of the session.

Your music/worship leader may choose to have a brief time of music.

The video presentation offers the content of the session, along with the corresponding chapter of *Habits of the Heart,* which participants can read either before or after the session. Before the video is shown, encourage everyone to follow along in the participant's guide. The participant's guide contains the biblical text for the session, room for notes about the presentation, and some questions designed to promote thought and discussion afterward.

After the video is shown, your director will invite everyone to break into the assigned small groups. Your task now begins in earnest. Use the gifts and skills we discussed in Chapter 2.

At the end of your discussion, close the conversation and end with prayer. Dismiss people from your small group without returning to the larger group.

At this point, the session is over and people may leave. Some persons will wish to remain and talk together, but no participant should be forced to stay beyond the announced ending time. All your leaders are to remain until all the participants have left. Then gather for a few moments to make plans for the next session.

HELPING INQUIRERS FOLLOW JESUS CHRIST

When you fulfill your role as a small-group leader and the Spirit of God is involved in the process, there is the possibility that participants in your small group may seriously consider redirecting their life toward Jesus Christ. This is the ultimate goal of the program. What you will discover is that the most satisfying and terrifying moment for any leader and host of *The Spiritual Life* is when a participant asks, "How can I become a Christian? How can I follow Jesus?" When a participant asks such questions, you have the opportunity to witness a new birth in Christ. These opportunities will come when you have trusting relationships with participants. When you express a clear, non-manipulative interest in a participant, not as a number but as a person, the conversation will get more serious. The participants watch you every week—what you say, how you act, and where your loyalties lie. When participants see in you a lifestyle that is attractive, they will want to live that way themselves. Participants who find your walk with Jesus Christ intriguing and compelling will want to go further. As your dialogue continues, you must be willing to assist them in understanding Jesus Christ as the true guide. When participants have this experience, we believe that Jesus Christ through the Holy Spirit is inviting them to redirect their life. Jesus Christ is always knocking on the door of our hearts. Your goal is to help participants hear the knock and discern God's call in their lives.

We believe that you can be like Jesus and lead people to living water. The following is an example of how you might lead someone to Jesus:

HOW CAN I BEGIN AN INTENTIONAL JOURNEY WITH JESUS CHRIST?
How Can I Become a Christian?

Being a Christian means following Jesus Christ. How does that happen? Do you know the story of Jesus' encounter with Nicodemus in John 3? Nicodemus was a good man who was looking for the meaning of life. Nicodemus probably fasted twice a week, prayed in the Temple in Jerusalem, gave his money away generously, and even taught religion at the religious academy. Yet with all these good deeds, he was still looking for direction in his journey. Jesus said to Nicodemus, "You must be born again" (John 3:7).

Because from the moment of birth all human beings are on a spiritual journey, the question is not, "When will you begin your walk with Jesus Christ?" Jesus Christ has always been walking beside you. Rather, the major question is, "Are you ready to begin an intentional, deliberate, and disciplined journey with Jesus Christ?" You have to choose which road to travel. Christians are the people who choose to walk along the way with Jesus Christ. How do you decide? How can you begin?

For each person, the answer is different. In the New Testament and throughout history, each of Jesus' followers came to him differently. Stories of redirection toward Jesus often have more differences than similarities. There is no simple formula, no cookie cutter recipe, no one road map, and no magic words. But all Christians have made a choice to follow Jesus Christ.

Can you choose to follow Jesus Christ today? Of course you can. Should you choose today? That is for you to decide. But if you want to walk down Jesus' path, one way to go is simply to say several very simple words to Jesus Christ. They begin as follows:

1. **"Thank you, God,"** for your love. Jesus said to Nicodemus, "God so loved the world that God gave God's only Son, so that everyone who believes in Jesus Christ may not perish but may have eternal life" (John 3:16; author's translation). You too have to acknowledge God as your loving Parent. Open your eyes, ears, and heart to see Jesus Christ coming to you and embracing you.

2. **"I'm sorry" that I have not been following your way.** Jesus began his ministry by telling everyone, "Turn around and believe in the good news" (Mark 1:15; author's translation). If you have been walking down another road, you must admit that you have not been walking with Jesus Christ.

3. **"Redirect me," and help me follow Jesus Christ in every step I take.** As Peter, another New Testament writer said, "Follow in his [Jesus'] steps" (1 Peter 2:21) and "For 'you were like sheep going astray,' but now you have returned to the Shepherd" (1 Peter 2:25). Say to Jesus Christ, "Jesus, be my companion and guide; point me in the right direction."

4. **"Let's start" the journey today.** As Paul said to some early Christians, "Now is the day of salvation" (2 Corinthians 6:2). Jesus Christ can become your guide today. "If you declare with your mouth, 'Jesus is Lord,' and believe in your heart that God raised him [Jesus] from the dead, you will be saved" (Romans 10:9). You may choose a new road to travel right now.

It is that simple.

These four phrases—Thank you, I'm sorry, redirect me, let's start—may take the form of a private conversation with God, such as,

"O loving God, I'm sorry about the roads I have traveled. I want to travel with Jesus today. Amen."

or

"Almighty God, I've made some wrong turns and am far from where I need to be. Jesus, guide me now. Amen."

or

"Jesus, I'm sorry. Why don't you take over now? Amen."

These four steps may also take place during a conversation with a Christian friend or another participant in or leader of *The Spiritual Life.* There are people around you in this program who would love to talk with you about following Jesus Christ. Just ask someone you trust.

Meeting Jesus Christ requires making room for him in your life and claiming him as your Guide and Shepherd along the way. Jesus Christ always comes to you. The appropriate response at each moment is to go to him. Despite your doubts, your fears, your denials, you simply have to say "Yes" to Jesus Christ. This new relationship depends on your listening, repenting, and trusting and on being empowered by Jesus Christ. As Jesus told his disciples, "I no longer call you servants. . . . Instead, I have called you friends" (John 15:15).

For some further reading about how to assist people in their journey, see *The Faith-Sharing New Testament With the Psalms,* by Eddie Fox and George Morris (Cokesbury in cooperation with Thomas Nelson, 1994). This book provides some additional resources about how to be a faithful companion to people considering becoming intentional Christians. Being a spiritual guide for a new birth is one of the highest privileges of being a follower of Jesus Christ. As a leadership team member you must not back away from such an opportunity but claim it as a gift from God.

Part Two:

Leading
The Spiritual Life

Session Outlines
for Small-Group Leaders

Session 1:
Where Is the Spirit
in Spirituality?

Introduction to the Spiritual Life

INTRODUCTION

Jesus Christ himself was on a spiritual journey that began in a desert. Like Native Americans on Vision Quests, Christians believe that the Holy Spirit is always present and guiding spiritual seekers. In this session we discuss how to be caught up by the Spirit of God.

PREPARATION

Prepare yourself spiritually. Pray for yourself and for all the participants.
Review these small-group leader's notes.
Read Chapter 1 in *Habits of the Heart: A Participant's Companion*.
Prepare the area where your small group will meet. Put out pencils/pens.

OPENING HOSPITALITY

Do not greet participants at the door. Stay at your assigned meal table to greet members of your small group, and introduce your small-group members to one another.
Ask participants to introduce themselves to persons at your table by telling one important thing about themselves that no one at the table knows.

SERVE THE MEAL

WELCOME *(5 minutes by director)*

SINGING *(5 minutes by music/worship leader)*

VIDEO/DVD PRESENTATION 1 *(20 minutes)*

DISCUSSION *(45 minutes by small-group leader)*

Prepare the chairs for small-group discussion. Put out pencils/pens if you have not already done so.

Pass around the "Contact Sheet" for the first time. Remind participants that this information will be used only under special circumstances.

Speak about the issue of confidentiality. Remind everyone that what is shared in the small group should stay in the small group.

Group Questions

1. Who are you? Introduce yourself briefly to the others in your group.

2. In what ways do you see people seeking spiritual fulfillment today? What thoughts, comments, or questions do you have about those ways?

3. Rob talked about his spiritual search. Where have you looked to satisfy your own spiritual yearnings?

4. Have you ever had an experience in which you became unexpectedly aware of God's presence? If so, describe the experience and its meaning for you.

5. What would it mean to allow yourself to be led by the Holy Spirit?

Weekly Reflection

Think of the occasions when you have been aware of God's presence in your life. Is there anything that these experiences share in common (people, places, circumstances, or feelings)?

Weekly Exercise

Fly a kite, hang a flag or windsock, take a hot air balloon ride, or go windsurfing. If all else fails, pretend you are a dog and stick your head out of the window of a car. Do something that helps you be attentive to the power of wind all around us.

A New Way of Praying
Breath Prayer

The Breath Prayer is a short, silent prayer that helps you become more aware of the Holy Spirit. You can use this prayer throughout the day as a way continually to experience the presence of the Spirit.

1. Sit for a moment in silence and remember that God is intimately present in your life. Remember that the Holy Spirit is as close as your next breath.
2. Now take a few moments to consider what you most want to ask God. Be honest. Simply tell God what is in your heart. Write or say your prayer in a short sentence. Example: "Holy Spirit, help me to remember that you love me."
3. Shorten your prayer to just six-to-eight syllables. Example: "Spirit, let me feel your love."
4. Close your eyes and breathe deeply for the next few minutes. Each time you exhale, concentrate on the words of your prayer.
5. Carry these words in your heart throughout the day. Every so often take a deep breath and then exhale while focusing on the words of the prayer. Gradually, whenever you are aware of your breathing, you will be reminded of these words. Your prayer will feel like a part of you, as natural as breath itself.

*　*　*

For further explorations into the Holy Spirit and spirituality, we invite you to read Chapter 1 in *Habits of the Heart*. Jesus Christ himself was on a spiritual journey that began in a wilderness. Like Native Americans on Vision

Quests, Christians believe that the Holy Spirit is always present and is always guiding spiritual seekers. As we move through the study, we will describe how you can become more open to the guidance of the Holy Spirit in your own life.

CLOSING *(5 minutes by small-group leader)*

Remind everyone about the schedule for next week, and make other necessary announcements.

Pass around the "Contact Sheet" for the first time, if you have not already done so. Remind participants that this information will be used only under special circumstances. Invite the participants to pause for a minute of silence to reflect on this session.

Pray together.

Adjourn on time.

SPECIAL NOTE

After the participants have left, meet with the members of your leadership team briefly to review the first session and to identify any corrections you need to make for the next session. Turn in the "Contact Sheet" to your director.

Session 2:
How Much
Am I Willing to Risk?

The Spiritual Habit of Courage

INTRODUCTION

Through the story of Jesus calling his first disciples (Mark 1:16-20 and Luke 5:1-11), we discover that risk is a necessary part of spiritual growth. In this session we seek to leave behind the fears that lead to the habit of cocooning and to develop the new spiritual habit of courage.

PREPARATION

Prepare yourself spiritually. Pray for yourself and for all the participants.
Review these small-group leader's notes.
Read Chapter 2 in *Habits of the Heart: A Participant's Companion.*
Prepare the area where the small group will meet.

Special Note: Practice the "directed reading" a few
times so that you feel comfortable leading Question 4.

OPENING HOSPITALITY

Welcome all participants.
Ask people to introduce themselves further at your table to other persons in their small group.

SERVE THE MEAL

WELCOME *(5 minutes by director)*

SINGING *(5 minutes by music/worship leader)*

VIDEO/DVD PRESENTATION 2 *(20 minutes)*

DISCUSSION *(45 minutes by small-group leader)*

Greet each member of your small group.

Pass around the "Contact Sheet" for the last time; from this point on, it will be used only under special circumstances. At the end of the session, give it to the director.

Remind everyone about confidentiality. What is said within the small group should stay within the small group.

Group Questions

1. Describe risks you have taken in your life—foolish risks as well as worthwhile risks. What were the results of those risks? What did you learn?

2. Name a person you would describe as having the courage to go deeper in life. (She or he may be someone you know or a famous person you have never met.) How did the person display courage?

3. What would you want to be said in your eulogy?

4. Your group leader will lead you in a "directed reading" of Mark 1:16-20. [Read this passage slowly, calmly yet with enthusiasm. Where you see ellipses, pause for about five seconds.]

Close your eyes. . . . Relax your arms. Your fingers. Your shoulders. Your stomach. Your legs. . . . Take a few slow, deep breaths. . . . Imagine that you are a fisherman, sitting in your boat repairing fishing nets. . . . Feel the warmth of the sun on your back. . . . As the gentle waves rock your boat back and forth, relax as you go about your work. . . . Hear Jesus' voice . . . . "Come, follow me," he says. . . . Allow yourself to feel the weight of this calling. . . . How do you feel? . . . Are you anxious? Afraid? Do you feel ready for something new? (pause for about twenty seconds)

Now, put down your fishing net. . . . Climb out of the boat. . . . Wade to the shore by Jesus' side. . . . Ask any questions that you want. . . . Express any feelings you have. . . . Listen to what Jesus tells you. . . . Become aware of any new feelings in your heart (pause for about one minute). When you feel ready, slowly open your eyes.

5. In what ways have you sensed the Holy Spirit leading you on a spiritual quest this week? You may want to refer to your weekly reflection, weekly exercise, experience with the Breath Prayer, or reading of Chapter 1 in *Habits of the Heart.*

Weekly Reflection

Reflect on your life by responding to the following questions:

• What risk did you take that made the most positive difference in your life?
• What do you regret not doing because you were afraid?
• Where have you displayed courage in your life?
• Where in your life do you wish you had put more energy and effort?
• Where should you have invested less of your energy?
• What is one thing you could change to help you move forward in your spiritual quest?

Weekly Exercise

Write your own obituary. A typical obituary appearing in the newspaper lists age at time of death, surviving family members, and significant life accomplishments. In addition, make your obituary more personal. Consider the person you hope to become—what you would like to do and how you would like to be remembered.

A New Way of Praying
Lectio Divina

In the Middle Ages, Benedictine monks would read the Bible together in groups in much the same way that your group read the story of Jesus calling his first disciples. The monks called this *Lectio Divina* (Latin for "sacred reading"). Lectio Divina can also be used for the personal prayers of an individual.

The goal of Lectio Divina is to "pray" the Scriptures in order to allow our deepest concerns to intertwine with the stories we read in the Bible. In Lectio Divina, we become more intentional about making connections between a biblical story and our lives.

Practice Lectio Divina with Mark 1:16-20.

1. Find a comfortable, quiet place. Sit in silence for a couple of minutes. Read Mark 16:1-20 slowly. Do not read the passage for information (as you would a newspaper). Instead, read the story like poetry, allowing the beauty of the words and the power of the story to shine through. Savor each portion of the reading. Pray that the Holy Spirit will speak to you through the story. Sit for a moment in silence. Now read the passage again. Listen for the Spirit. A particular word or phrase or event in the story may speak to your heart. If not, try reading it slowly one more time.
2. When a word or phrase seems to speak to you, stop reading. Take that word or phrase into your heart. Repeat it to yourself slowly and quietly.
3. Take a few moments to consider why the Holy Spirit may have directed your attention to this part of the story. How does it connect to your life? Does it speak to your fears? Does it suggest a risk that makes you uneasy or excited?
4. Finally, rest in the presence of the Holy Spirit. Try turning the word or phrase into a Breath Prayer, repeating your new prayer for a few moments.

* * *

For further explorations into fear, risk, and the spiritual habit of courage, we invite you to read Chapter 2 in *Habits of the Heart*. This chapter examines reasons why we all sometimes avoid risks we should take. It explores the fears of change and failure that so often paralyze us and offers advice on how we can spread our wings and leave fear behind us.

CLOSING *(5 minutes by small-group leader)*

Remind everyone about the schedule for next week, and make other necessary announcements.

Pass around the "Contact Sheet" for the last time, if you have not already done so. Remind participants that this information will be used only under special circumstances.

Invite the participants to pause for a minute of silence to reflect on this session. Pray together.

Adjourn on time.

Session 3:
What Is Most Important to Me?

The Spiritual Habit of Loving

INTRODUCTION

Following Jesus Christ calls for a different way of living that focuses on loving God and loving other people. This spiritual habit of the heart helps us overcome the loneliness and narcissism that often separates us from God and others.

PREPARATION

Prepare yourself spiritually. Pray for yourself and for all the participants.
Review these small-group leader's notes.
Read Chapter 3 in *Habits of the Heart: A Participant's Companion.*

Prepare the area where your small group will meet.

The pattern each week will include the meal, the welcome, singing, and the video/DVD presentation.

DISCUSSION *(45 minutes by small-group leader)*
+Greet each member of your small group.

Group Questions

1. Which one of Rob's stories spoke to you most deeply about love? Why?

2. Name someone who loved you well. Describe how he or she loved you.

3. Name someone whom you loved well. Describe how you loved her or him.

4. In what ways have you sensed the Holy Spirit leading you in your spiritual quest this week? You may want to refer to your weekly reflection, weekly exercise, experience with Lectio Divina, or reading of Chapter 2 in *Habits of the Heart.*

Weekly Reflection

Each of the stories Rob told illustrated a person's giftedness, the leading of the Holy Spirit, and someone's needs in a specific situation. Love was revealed in the intersection of these three forces. Consider your gifts and the promptings of the Holy Spirit. Can you think of an occasion, a place, or a situation where you may love?

Weekly Exercise

Try improving your "love life" this week by experimenting with one or more of these simple expressions of love:

• Slip a love note into your spouse's briefcase or your child's lunch box.
• Write a note of encouragement to a struggling friend.
• Call a member of your extended family or an old friend. Tell that person how much he or she has meant to you throughout your life.
• Go to a crowded shopping mall or public park and watch the people. Think of how much and in what ways God loves the people you see.

A New Way of Praying
Prayer of Adoration

Many Christians use the Book of Psalms in their personal prayers. From this Old Testament prayer book, you can find poetic words to suit almost any emotion or occasion. One of the most prevalent themes in the Book of Psalms is the adoration of God. A prayer of adoration is a simple expression of your love for God. Move into a kneeling position with the palms of your hands facing up. Now repeat these words from Psalm 8:

> O LORD, Our Sovereign,
> how majestic is your name in all the earth!

You have set your glory above the heavens. . . .

When I look at your heavens,
    the work of your fingers,
    the moon and the stars that you have established;
what are human beings that you are mindful of them,
    mortals that you care for them?

Yet you have made them a little lower than God,
    and crowned them with glory and honor. . . .

O LORD, our Sovereign,
    how majestic is your name in all the earth!
                    (Psalm 8: 1-5, 9)

*   *   *

For further explorations into these and other questions, we invite you to read Chapter 3 in *Habits of the Heart*. The chapter defines love in terms of God's deep, abiding affection for every creature. It asks why love is sometimes difficult for us and explores the challenges of isolation and narcissism. Finally, the chapter suggests how we can fully experience God's love and begin to share that love with others.

CLOSING *(5 minutes by small-group leader)*

Remind everyone about the schedule for next week, and make other necessary announcements.

Invite the participants to pause for a minute of silence to reflect on this session.

Pray together.

Adjourn on time.

Session 4:
Can I Find Balance
in a Whirlwind World?

The Spiritual Habit of Centering

INTRODUCTION

Through the story of Mary and Martha, we discover how difficult it can be
to keep our balance in this hectic, demanding world and how the habit of
centering helps us recover the balance that we have lost.

PREPARATION

Prepare yourself spiritually. Pray for yourself and for all the participants.
Review these small-group leader's notes.
Read Chapter 4 in *Habits of the Heart: A Participant's Companion.*
Prepare the area where your small group will meet.

DISCUSSION *(45 minutes by small-group leader)*

Greet each member of your small group.

Group Questions

1. What day this week did you feel most hurried, pressured, or out of balance? Describe the experience.

2. In his presentation, Rob talked about how he sometimes becomes overwhelmed in the midst of multi-tasking. How do you respond when you have to multi-task? What is your reaction when you feel overwhelmed?

3. What are the occasions (when and where) that you feel most centered?

4. Rob talked about kayaking in the wind and being unable to move in the right direction until he learned to drop the skeg (the stabilizing keel) into the water. What is your skeg? How do you extend your life into the depths so that the wind does not buffet you on the surface?

5. In what ways have you sensed the Holy Spirit leading you on your spiritual quest this week? You may want to refer to your weekly reflection, weekly exercise, experience with praying the psalms, or reading of Chapter 3 in *Habits of the Heart.*

Weekly Reflection

When your world spins out of balance, how do you become centered? What are some additional strategies you have not yet tried that you might try? Do you recall Jesus' centering responses that Rob discussed? How might these fit into your life?

Weekly Exercise

To practice a centering activity, make a loaf of bread the old-fashioned way. (No electric bread makers allowed!)

Bread Recipe *(makes 2 loaves)*

2 packages active dry yeast
¾ cup warm water
2⅔ cups warm water
¼ cup sugar
3 tablespoons shortening
9–10 cups flour

Dissolve yeast in ¾ cup warm water. Stir in the additional 2⅔ cups warm water, along with the sugar, salt, shortening, and 5 cups of flour. Beat until smooth. Mix in enough of the remaining flour to make the dough easy to handle.

Turn the dough on a lightly floured board. Knead until smooth and elastic (about 10 minutes). Punch down dough. Divide in half. Roll each half into a rectangle (about 18 x 9 inches). Roll up, beginning at the short side. Fold ends under. Place seam side down in greased loaf pan (9 x 5 x 3 inches). Brush lightly with melted butter. Let the bread rise in a warm space until the size doubles (about 1 hour).

Heat oven to 425 degrees. Place loaves on low rack so that tops of pans are in the center of the oven. Bake 30–35 minutes or until loaves are deep golden brown and loaves sound hollow when tapped. Remove from pans. Brush loaves with soft butter.

Enjoy!

A New Way of Praying
Centering Prayer

Since the days of the early church, Christians have used Centering Prayer to reestablish balance in their lives and to develop a more intimate relationship with the Holy Spirit.

Centering Prayer is a method of intentional silence and stillness to bring the distracted, unbalanced heart back to its true focus on God. Buddhist monks jokingly describe the problem of "monkey mind" when our attention jumps from one thing to the next like a monkey jumping from tree to tree. Practice Centering Prayer each day this week. It is a great cure for "monkey mind."

In Centering Prayer, you will spend a certain amount of time (usually fifteen-to-twenty minutes a day) meditating on a "sacred word" such as Spirit, Jesus, peace, or shalom (the Hebrew word for peace). At first, try ten minutes of Centering Prayer.

1. Find a comfortable chair and sit with your eyes closed and your body relaxed.
2. Remind yourself of your intention by repeating this short passage from Psalm 46:10a several times: "Be still, and know that I am God!"
3. Centering Prayer actually begins as you say the sacred word you have chosen. Use one of the words suggested above or another one- or two-syllable word that has special meaning for you. Repeat this word in the

silence of your mind in a calm, slow, and gentle rhythm. Your goal is not to think of the meaning of this word but to use it as a symbol of your willingness to lay all your other concerns aside and focus on God.

4. Whenever an emotion, image, or thought enters your mind, try to put it aside. Eventually you will not even need to say your sacred word. It will simply drop from your mind. You do not need to do anything to make this happen. As the word drops away, your attentiveness to God grows deeper.

5. After ten minutes have elapsed, close your prayer by saying, "Amen."

* * *

For further explorations into how to have a more centered life, we invite you to read Chapter 4 in *Habits of the Heart*. This chapter discusses some of the reasons why life gets out of balance. By teaching you the spiritual habit of centering, the chapter shows how you can begin to develop a gentler, more gracious life modeled after Jesus Christ.

CLOSING *(5 minutes by small-group leader)*

Remind everyone about the schedule for next week, and make other necessary announcements.

Invite the participants to pause for a minute of silence to reflect on this session.

Pray together.

Adjourn on time.

Session 5:
What Do I Want to Be When I Grow Up?

The Spiritual Habit of Simplicity

INTRODUCTION

In the midst of cluttered lives, developing the habit of simplicity helps us become more attentive to God and the people around us. Using the example of children, we focus on spiritual priorities.

PREPARATION

Prepare yourself spiritually. Pray for yourself and for all the participants.
Review these small-group leader's notes.
Read Chapter 5 in *Habits of the Heart: A Participant's Companion.*
Prepare the area where the small group will meet.
Buy crayons for Question 1. Ask participants to write their responses to this question in crayon.

DISCUSSION *(45 minutes by small-group leader)*

Greet each member of your small group.

Group Questions

1. Using crayons, list the top five attributes you most admire in children.

2. When you were a child, how did you answer the question, "What do you want to be when you grow up?" How did you do?

3. Rob recalled how seeing the Grand Canyon changed the scale of his perspective. What similar experience have you had?

4. In what ways have you sensed the Holy Spirit leading you on your spiritual quest this week? You may want to refer to your weekly reflection, weekly exercise, experience with Centering Prayer, or reading of Chapter 4 in *Habits of the Heart.*

Weekly Reflection

What could you do to simplify your life? Write down four changes that you feel might help.

1._____
2._____
3._____
4._____

Circle the change that is most important to begin now.

Weekly Exercise

During the next six days, experiment with incorporating into your life one of the following simplifying habits:

• Go one day without watching television.
• Cut up one credit card.
• Go to the library and read a book.
• Play with a child.
• Choose to shop at a local retail store rather than at a megamarket.
• Take a nap.
• Start a book club.
• Say no.
• For every piece of new clothing you purchase, give a comparable item from your wardrobe to charity.
• Ride public transportation.

A New Way of Praying
Prayer and Fasting

Fasting (abstaining from food) is not prayer, but it is a complement to prayer—a way to deepen your prayer life.

Throughout the Bible, you can find people experiencing extended periods of prayer and fasting. Moses, Elijah, and Jesus all endured forty days of fasting in the desert (Deuteronomy 9:9; 1 Kings 19:8; Luke 4:2).

Some contemporary Christians fast one day a month or even one day a week. Fasting takes practice. Add it to your prayer life slowly and gradually. A good way to start is with a partial fast, setting aside a day to abstain from one or two meals.

Try a partial fast one day this week, skipping breakfast or lunch.

1. For a couple of days before your fast, reduce your consumption of coffee and soft drinks. Suddenly abstaining from caffeinated drinks may cause withdrawal symptoms that could distract you from your prayers.
2. On the morning of your fast, begin by drinking some fruit juice. Throughout the day, drink several glasses of water to keep your body hydrated.
3. Live your day normally, trying not to draw attention to your fast. Allow it to be a personal, private matter shared between you and the Holy Spirit.
4. Devote the time you normally spend eating to practicing the prayers you have learned in the earlier weeks: Breath Prayer, Lectio Divina, Prayer of Adoration, and Centering Prayer.
5. Throughout your fast, allow your hunger pangs to be a silent call to prayer. Practice your Breath Prayer during these moments.
6. Break your fast with a light meal. Before you begin eating, pray the Lord's Prayer and pay special attention to the petition "Give us this day our daily bread." Allow these words to remind you how God takes care of you and provides for your physical and spiritual needs. Eat slowly, savoring each bite. Be aware of the physical pleasure of eating, and feel grateful.

* * *

For further explorations into simple living, we invite you to read Chapter 5 in *Habits of the Heart*. The chapter describes how, in the midst of cluttered lives, developing the habit of simplicity helps us become more attentive to God and the people around us. Using the example of children, we discuss how to set aside the clutter and begin to focus on spiritual priorities.

CLOSING *(5 minutes by small-group leader)*

Remind everyone about the schedule for next week, and make other necessary announcements.

Invite the participants to take their crayon home with them, perhaps carrying it in their pockets throughout the week as a visible reminder to be more childlike.

Invite the participants to pause for a minute of silence to reflect on this session.

Pray together.

Adjourn on time.

Session 6:
How Do I Keep My Possessions From Possessing Me?

The Spiritual Habit of Giving

INTRODUCTION

Our society is obsessed with materialism, substituting material possessions for holy relationships with God and others. In this session we discuss how to become dis-possessed from our possessions by the spiritual habit of giving.

PREPARATION

Prepare yourself spiritually. Pray for yourself and for all the participants.
Review these small-group leader's notes.
Read Chapter 6 in *Habits of the Heart: A Participant's Companion*.
Prepare the area where the small group will meet.

DISCUSSION *(45 minutes by small-group leader)*

Greet each member of your small group.

Group Questions

1. How many catalogs do you receive in the mail each week? Which is your favorite?

2. Name something you wasted your money on this week. Why was the purchase wasteful?

3. Describe an experience in which you gave money to a person or group. How did it make you feel?

4. Rob told about a girl who had been taught to divide her allowance into three equal boxes—for spending, saving, and giving away. Who taught you your attitude toward possessions? What were the lessons, and how were they communicated?

5. In what ways have you sensed the Holy Spirit leading you on your spiritual quest this week? You may want to refer to your weekly reflection, weekly exercise, experience with fasting, or reading of Chapter 5 in *Habits of the Heart.*

Weekly Reflection

Look back through your checkbook and credit card receipts. What does your spending tell you about the priorities in your life?

Weekly Exercise

Do you ever wonder where all your money goes? For the next week, create and use a "fritter finder" to help you see how you "fritter" some of your money away. Each day carry a small sheet of paper with two columns—one labeled "Item" and the next labeled "Cost." Write down every item you buy and how much it cost. Calculate the total at the end of the week.

• Were you surprised where the money went?
• Can you identify any purchases that seemed frivolous?
• Did the habit of writing down all your purchases slow down your spending or make you reconsider any of the purchases you made?

A New Way of Praying
Repetitive Prayer

Praying a brief Repetitive Prayer throughout the day is one way Christians can learn to "pray continually" (1 Thessalonians 5:17). In the video, Rob discussed how our possessions can gain power over us. Try repeating these words as a way to remind you where the source of your power is: "I can do all this through [Christ] who gives me strength" (Philippians 4:13). Read this verse prayerfully, each time emphasizing a different word.

1. *I* can do all this through Christ who gives me strength.
2. I *can* do all this through Christ who gives me strength.
3. I can *do* all this through Christ who gives me strength.
4. I can do *all* this through Christ who gives me strength.
5. I can do all *this* through Christ who gives me strength.
6. I can do all this *through* Christ who gives me strength.
7. I can do all this through *Christ* who gives me strength.
8. I can do all this through Christ *who* gives me strength.
9. I can do all this through Christ who *gives* me strength.
10. I can do all this through Christ who gives *me* strength.
11. I can do all this through Christ who gives me *strength*.

* * *

For further explorations into money, possessions, and the spiritual habit of giving, we invite you to read Chapter 6 in *Habits of the Heart*. The chapter describes how our society is obsessed with materialism, substituting material possessions for holy relationships with God and others, as well as how we can become "dis-possessed."

CLOSING *(5 minutes by small-group leader)*

Remind everyone about the schedule for next week, and make other necessary announcements.

Invite the participants to pause for a minute of silence to reflect on this session.

Pray together.

Adjourn on time.

Session 7:
How Do I Get Ahead?

The Spiritual Habit of Serving

INTRODUCTION

We live in a service economy, where everyone expects to be served. In opposition to our culture of entitlement, Jesus offers another habit of the heart: serving one another. Using the image of foot washing, in this session we discuss how to serve our neighbors in large ways, and small.

PREPARATION

Prepare yourself spiritually. Pray for yourself and for all the participants. Review these small-group leader's notes.
Read Chapter 7 in *Habits of the Heart: A Participant's Companion.*

DISCUSSION *(45 minutes by small-group leader)*

Greet each member of your small group.

Group Questions

1. Name an occasion this week when someone has been of service to you. How did it make you feel? How did you respond?

2. Name a recent occasion when you served someone. How did it make you feel? How did you respond?

3. Can you name a person in your life, such as the doctor in Rob's story, who has made an impression on you by the sacrifices he or she made for others? If so, describe that person and what the sacrifice was.

4. Is it harder for you to serve someone or to allow someone to serve you? Why?

5. In what ways have you sensed the Holy Spirit leading you on your spiritual quest this week? You may want to refer to your weekly reflection, weekly exercise, experience with the Repetitive Prayer, or reading of Chapter 6 in *Habits of the Heart.*

Weekly Reflection

Author and Presbyterian minister Frederick Buechner once gave some wise advice about service. He said that your unique arena of service is "the place where your deep gladness meets the world's deep need."[1]

As a way to reflect on Buechner's advice, complete the following statements:

Your Deep Gladness	**The World's Deep Need**
If I let myself admit it, I think I have a gift for _____.	My heart aches when I see someone suffering from _____.
If I did not have to worry about money, I would spend my life doing _____.	Of all the world's problems, the one that most concerns me is _____.

I feel best about myself when I help someone to _____.

Weekly Exercise

Rob talked about being a "ninja servant"—performing anonymous acts of service for other people. This week, try being a ninja servant.

A New Way of Praying
Covenant Prayer

Christians have used the Covenant Prayer for over two hundred years. The prayer urges Christians to renew their commitment to serve God and others at significant occasions in their life. Many contemporary Christians offer this prayer once a year or even once a month to reaffirm their covenant to make personal sacrifices in the name of Christ.

1. Kneel while folding your hands in front of you, or assume some other position that expresses humility before God.
2. Read the Covenant Prayer, pausing for a moment of silent reflection after each line:

Dear God,
I am no longer my own, but thine.
Put me to what thou wilt, rank me with whom thou wilt.
Put me to doing, put me to suffering.
Let me be employed by thee or laid aside by thee,
    exalted for thee or brought low by thee.
Let me be full, let me be empty.
I freely and heartily yield all things
    to thy pleasure and disposal.
And now . . . Father, Son, and Holy Spirit,
    thou art mine, and I am thine. So be it.
And the covenant which I have made on earth,
    let it be ratified in heaven. Amen.[2]

*　　*　　*

For further explorations into the habit of serving, we invite you to read Chapter 7 in *Habits of the Heart*. This chapter discusses our service economy, in which everyone expects to be served. In contrast to our culture of entitlement, Jesus offers another habit of the heart: serving one another. Using the image of foot washing, we discuss how to serve our neighbors in ways large and small.

CLOSING *(5 minutes by small-group leader)*

Remind everyone about the schedule for next week, and make other necessary announcements.

Invite the participants to pause for a minute of silence to reflect on this session.

Pray together.

Adjourn on time.

---

1. From *Wishful Thinking: A Seeker's ABC,* by Frederick Buechner (HarperCollins, 1993); page 119.
2. From "A Covenant Prayer in the Wesleyan Tradition," in *The United Methodist Hymnal* (Copyright © 1989 by The United Methodist Publishing House); 607. Used by permission.

Session 8:
Can I Go Deeper Without Going Under?

The Spiritual Habit of Trusting

INTRODUCTION

Once we become adults, we seem to have a difficult time trusting other people and God. In this session we explore the roots of mistrust and how we can begin to develop the spiritual habit of trusting.

PREPARATION

Prepare yourself spiritually. Pray for yourself and for all the participants.
Review these small-group leader's notes.
Read Chapter 8 in *Habits of the Heart: A Participant's Companion.*
Prepare the area where your small group will meet.

DISCUSSION *(45 minutes by small-group leader)*

Greet each member of your small group.

Group Questions

1. Describe an experience when someone taught you how to swim, ride a bicycle, or drive an automobile. What did the experience teach you about trust?

2. What is your immediate reaction when someone says, "Trust me"? Why do you respond that way?

3. Do you remember Rob's story about the disciples in a boat during a storm? Have you ever had an experience when you felt like you were going under?

4. Are you more likely to say, "I'm fine" or "Help me"? Do you have a group with whom you can share your struggles? Could you go to God?

5. In what ways have you sensed the Holy Spirit leading you on your spiritual quest this week? You may want to refer to your weekly reflection, weekly exercise, experience with the Covenant Prayer, or reading of Chapter 7 in *Habits of the Heart.*

Weekly Reflection

Sociologist Peter Berger says that people learn to trust God through their childhood relationships with their parents. He points to the example of a mother comforting her child who awakens, terrified, from a nightmare. Berger writes, "She will turn on a lamp, perhaps, which will encircle the scene with a warm glow of reassuring light. She will speak or sing . . . and the content of this communication will invariably be . . . 'Don't be afraid—everything is in order, everything is all right.'" Berger concludes that not only will the child be reassured; the child may also begin to believe that God, the Parent of us all, can be trusted.[1]

Recall an incident in your childhood when you were filled with trust for your parents. Try to remember every detail you can about the experience. What happened? What did your parents say? What did they do? Describe as fully as possible how you felt.

Now imagine that God can provide the same sense of assurance you experienced at that moment. Does this exercise alter your understanding of God in any way?

Weekly Exercise

Pick a safe area and a moonlit night and then go for a walk without a flashlight. As you are walking, consider your moments of uncertainty. Do your gropings and small, tentative steps remind you of your spiritual quest? What other insights did you have from the experience?

A New Way of Praying
Prayer Walk

A Prayer Walk supports your physical health and your spiritual health in the same activity. It reminds us that we are both body and soul. The goal of a Prayer Walk is to be more attentive to the world around us, allowing our surroundings to lead us deeper into prayer. When you come across some inspirational scene, you are immediately reminded of the love of our Creator.

1. Prepare yourself spiritually for the walk. Take a deep breath and exhale. Allow your muscles to feel relaxed and loose.
2. Choose a path where you will feel safe and secure.
3. Try to walk more slowly than your usual pace. Take deep, even breaths.
4. Be attentive to beauty wherever you find it. When you see something inspiring, pause, focus your attention, and say a short prayer of thanksgiving.

*   *   *

For further explorations into this issue, we invite you to read Chapter 8 in *Habits of the Heart.* Sometimes faith is seen as a personal quality that only a fortunate few possess. This chapter suggests that faith is available to everyone. Faith is simply learning to trust God. We overcome distrust in our lives, beginning to rely less on ourselves and more on God.

CLOSING *(5 minutes by small-group leader)*

Remind everyone about the schedule for next week, and make other necessary announcements.

Invite the participants to pause for a minute of silence to reflect on this session.

Pray together.

Adjourn on time.

---

1. From *A Rumor of Angels: Modern Society and the Rediscovery of the Supernatural,* 2nd expanded edition, by Peter Berger (Doubleday Anchor Books, 1990); pages 61–62.

Session 9:
What Do I Do
With My Doubts?

The Spiritual Habit of Questioning

INTRODUCTION

Sometimes Christians feel that they must be certain of their beliefs in order to "qualify" as a follower of Jesus. In this session we counter this assumption. We insist that questioning is not only a natural part of the spiritual life, it is an important habit of the heart that should be cultivated for spiritual growth to occur.

PREPARATION

Prepare yourself spiritually. Pray for yourself and for all the participants.
Review these small-group leader's notes.
Read Chapter 9 in *Habits of the Heart: A Participant's Companion.*
Prepare the area where the small group will meet.

DISCUSSION *(45 minutes by small-group leader)*

Greet each member of your small group.

Group Questions

1. Where and when did you learn to dance? What was the experience like?

2. Rob talked about three of his friends:

   • a young woman who had built a comfortable system of faith that she thought protected her and then awakened to the possibility that her house of belief was preventing her from experiencing a larger reality

- a college student who felt his faith challenged by religion classes; what he believed to be true was threatened
- a church visitor who saw his only option as choosing between faith and reason

Have you ever had an experience like any of these? If so, what was it like for you?

3. Have you ever doubted the love of someone in your life and then discovered those doubts to be unfounded? Do you think this could be true in your relationship with God?

4. In what ways have you sensed the Holy Spirit leading you in your spiritual quest this week? You may want to refer to your weekly reflection, weekly exercise, experience with the Prayer Walk, or reading of Chapter 8 in *Habits of the Heart*.

Weekly Reflection

Think about all the spiritual habits we have discussed: courage, loving, centering, simplicity, giving, serving, trusting, questioning. Be prepared to share with your group which one of these you especially want to adopt.

Weekly Exercise

Find a friend (perhaps someone in your study group) and discuss together a question that each of you has about Christianity.

A New Way of Praying
Welcoming Prayer

Welcoming Prayer grows out of Centering Prayer. The goal of Welcoming Prayer is to accept questions, doubts, and transitions within the context of your relationship with the Holy Spirit.

1. Spend about fifteen minutes reflecting on the doubts or persistent questions that accompany your spiritual life. Focus your attention on them.
2. Follow the pattern of Centering Prayer. First, find a comfortable chair and sit with your eyes closed and your body relaxed.

3. Repeat your sacred word—such as Jesus, Spirit, peace, or shalom (the Hebrew word for peace)—in a calm, slow, gentle rhythm.
4. Invite your questions or doubts into your heart. You may want to say, "I welcome my questions." Repeat this sentence, knowing that you are held up by a God who is greater than your doubts.
5. When you begin to feel comfortable in the presence of your doubts, close your prayer with the affirmation, "I do believe; help me, Holy Spirit, to overcome my unbelief."

*   *   *

For further explorations into the spiritual challenge of doubt, we invite you to read Chapter 9 in *Habits of the Heart*. We offer advice about how to respond to the presence of doubts in our lives. Rather than repressing our doubts, we encourage one another to appreciate doubts as a valuable part of our searching.

CLOSING *(5 minutes by small-group leader)*

Remind everyone about the schedule for next week, and make other necessary announcements.

Remind participants that they will be invited to share their weekly reflection with the group next week.

Invite the participants to pause for a minute of silence to reflect on this session.

Pray together.

Adjourn on time.

SPECIAL NOTES

Pass out the participant questionnaires, and ask participants to fill them out and return them at the next session.

Take home and fill out your small-group leader evaluation of each participant in your group, as well as your small-group leader questionaire. Turn them in to your director next week.

Complete your small-group leader questionnaire, and turn it in to your director.

Session 10:
Can a Change in Me Change the World?

The Spiritual Habit of Engaging

INTRODUCTION

Can one small change in your life make a difference in our world? Just as Jesus' life changed society, so too can our simple acts that imitate him initiate small changes that through the power of the Holy Spirit begin to change the world. In this session we discuss how each one of us may become a catalyst for change in our families, our community, and even our world.

PREPARATION

Prepare yourself spiritually. Pray for yourself and for all the participants.
Review these small-group leader's notes.
Read Chapter 10 in *Habits of the Heart: A Participant's Companion*.
Prepare the area where the small group will meet.

DISCUSSION *(45 minutes by small-group leader)*

Greet each member of your small group.

Group Questions

1. What brought you to this class? What has been your experience in the class?

2. Which spiritual habit has stirred your heart most deeply during the past weeks? Why? How will you put this spiritual habit into practice?

3. In what ways have you sensed the Holy Spirit leading you in your spiritual quest this week? You may want to refer to your weekly reflection, weekly exercise, experience with the Welcoming Prayer, or reading of Chapter 9 in *Habits of the Heart.*

Weekly Reflection

Review again the whole study. What did you learn about yourself? What did you learn about the other people in your group? What did you learn about God? How have you been led by the Holy Spirit to change?

Weekly Exercise

Choose one, two, or three habits that you will observe in the days to come. Write down the habit(s) on a slip of paper or post-note and place it on your refrigerator. Then let the Holy Spirit guide you to develop the habit(s).

A New Way of Praying
Benediction

A Benediction is typically associated with the close of a service of worship. The worship leader offers a short blessing sending the worshipers out into the world to have new experiences of the Holy Spirit. Share any prayer request you have for help on your spiritual quest. Each participant is invited to offer a short blessing, sending one another out into the world to change and to be changed by the Holy Spirit.

* * *

For further explorations into the spiritual habit of engaging, we invite you to read Chapter 10 in *Habits of the Heart.* In that chapter we ask, "Can one small change in my life make a difference in the world?" Just as Jesus himself changed society, so too can our simple acts, in his name, initiate small changes that may transform the world.

CLOSING *(5 minutes by small-group leader)*

Thank everyone for participating.

Collect the "Participant Questionnaires" and turn in to the director.

Also turn in your "Small-Group Leader Questionnaire" and "Small-Group Leader Evaluation of Participants."

Make other necessary announcements.

Invite the participants to pause for a minute of silence to reflect on this session.

Pray together.

Adjourn on time.

Say goodbye.